Creating with Collage

by Deborah Schecter

Contents

Get Ready for Collage! 2

GREAT SHAPES
Silly Scrambles 4
Heart-to-heart Match-up........6
Loop and Swoop.........................8
Torn Paper Picture.................10

LET'S GO TO THE CIRCUS!
Circus Train.............................12
Jumping Clown..........................14
Friendly Lion 16
High-wire Act..........................18
Up, Up, and Away!...................20

FEATHERED FRIENDS
Wonderful Woven Egg...........22
Whirly Birdies.......................24
Purdy Bird Mask.....................26

HOME, SWEET HOME
Happy Hats.............................28
Cozy Collage Quilt..................30

More Fun with Collage!.............32

Scholastic Inc.
New York Toronto London Auckland Sydney Mexico City New Delhi Hong Kong Buenos Aires

Get Ready for Collage!

Dear Young Artist,

How would you like to ride on a circus train or in a hot-air balloon? Now you can! All you have to do is snip, snip, cut, and glue. This book has a bunch of fun-filled collage projects—just for you!

Dear Parent,

Cutting out shapes from paper and arranging them to make a collage is a creative and fun experience for young children. As with many art projects, your child will also benefit by strengthening the fine motor skills needed in writing.

Deborah

Collage Tips

1. Spread newspaper on the surface where you will work.

2. You have two kinds of glue in your pack: a glue stick and school glue. Use the glue stick for gluing one piece of paper to another. Use the school glue to make heavy things like buttons and beads stick to your collage. Just a dab of glue will do the trick.

3. Use damp paper towels to wipe glue from your fingers.

4. Save those scraps! Don't throw away bits and pieces of leftover paper from your projects. You can use them when you make a new collage!

5. Besides your construction paper pad, you can use lots of other materials in your collage projects: gift wrap, aluminum foil, tissue paper, pictures from old magazines, cardboard, buttons, beads, yarn, ribbon, dried beans, and pasta! What other materials can you think of?

6. To make a bigger collage picture, you can glue your collage cutouts to a larger sheet of construction paper.

Collage Techniques

Folding Paper folded the short way looks like this.

Paper folded the long way looks like this.

Curling Tightly wind a strip of paper around a pencil. Then remove the pencil.

Fringes Cut lots of slits, side by side. Be careful not to cut all the way through the paper.

Pleating Starting at one end of a strip of paper, make a fold. Crease the fold with your thumb. Then turn the paper over, and fold the paper back in the opposite direction. Keep folding back and forth until you reach the end of the paper.

Zigzag Cut thin strips from a pleated piece of paper.

Spiral Cut out a circle. Then, starting at one edge, cut around and around the circle, moving toward the middle. When you're almost at the center, stop cutting.

Silly Scrambles

All you need are a few simple shapes to make this cool collage.

  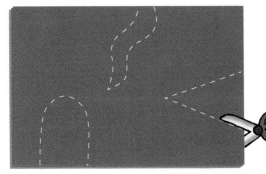

1. Pick three sheets of paper of different colors. Line them up together.

2. Keeping the sheets together, cut out different shapes from your paper.

3. You can make squares, rectangles, triangles, or any shape you like.

4. Pick another sheet of colored pape Try different ways of placing your cutouts on the paper. Overlap some of the shapes, if you like.

5. When you like how your design looks, use your glue stick to glue your shapes to the paper. (Hint: Only take off one or two shapes at a time so you don't forget your design!)

For more fun with shapes, turn the page!

Heart-to-heart Match-up

What a great way to say I love you!

1. Pick a sheet of colored paper.

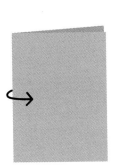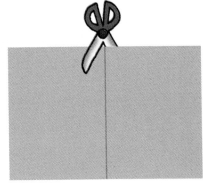

2. Fold the sheet in half the short way. Then unfold the paper and cut it in two along the crease. (Save one of the halves of paper for another project.)

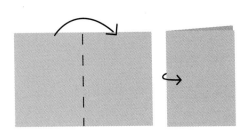

3. Now fold your half sheet of paper in half the short way again.

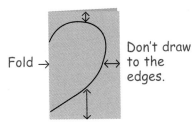

Fold → Don't draw to the edges.

4. Use a pencil to draw half of a heart shape on one side of the fold. Be careful not to draw all the way to the edges of your paper.

5. Starting from the fold, cut out your heart shape. Now you have two pieces: your half-heart shape and the paper you cut the shape from.

half-heart frames   half hearts

6. Unfold these pieces. Then cut each in half along the crease. Now you have four pieces: two half-heart frames and two half hearts.

7. It's time for your heart-to-heart match-up! Pick another sheet of colored paper. Turn it the tall way. Place each half heart on the paper so it faces one of the half-heart frames. When you like how the shapes look, glue them to your paper, using your glue stick.

Loop and Swoop

Fold, fringe, curl, and swirl. You can make paper do amazing things!

1. Pick two sheets of paper of different colors.

2. Cut each sheet of paper into strips. Make some wide strips and some thin ones.

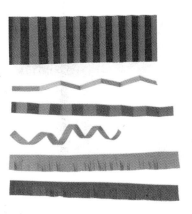

3. Try changing the strips in different ways. Make pleats, zigzags, curls, and fringes. (See page 3.)

4. Glue the end of one strip to a sheet of paper. Then do the same thing with a few more strips. Glue them to different parts of the paper.

5. Try twisting and looping the strips over and under one another. Make bridges and tunnels and stairs! Glue the other ends of the strips to the paper.

You won't need your scissors for the next project—but it's collage just the same!

Torn Paper Picture

Your fingers are the scissors for this project!

1. Think of a picture that you would like to make. Or just start tearing pieces of paper. You may get an idea from the shapes you make.

2. To tear paper into different shapes, hold the paper between your thumb and pointer finger of each hand. Then tear it slowly.

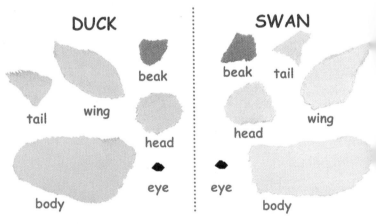

DUCK

beak

tail wing

head

body eye

SWAN

beak tail

head wing

eye body

3. To make the scene here, tear long blue pieces of paper for the water. Tear a long green piece for the grass. Place them on a sheet of paper.

4. To make a duck and a swan, tear a medium sized oval shape for each body and a small round shape for each head. Tear shapes for the wings and beak, as shown. Tear two small, black circle shapes for eyes.

5. To make a tree, tear a narrow black strip for the trunk. Tear a round green shape for the leaves. Add apples by tearing small pieces of red paper.

6. Tear a yellow sun and glue it in the corner of your picture. Add rays to your sun by tearing small yellow strips. What else would you like to add to your picture?

Circus Train

Hip, hip, hooray! The circus is coming to town!

What You Can Add:
dried pasta wheels   cotton balls

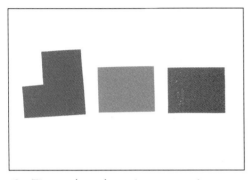

1. To make the circus train cars, cut rectangles out of different colors of paper. Make an engine, a train car, and a red caboose, too!

2. Arrange your train cars on a sheet of paper. Cut black strips to connect them. Then glue the pieces to the paper.

Train with pasta wheels

3. Ready for the wheels? You can use colored paper circles. Or you can use pasta wheels instead.

4. Add windows, a smokestack, and other parts to your train.

5. Make some steam using bits of white paper or cotton balls.

6. Decorate your train with even more shapes and colors!

Who's waiting to welcome you to the circus? Turn the page to see!

Jumping Clown

Look who's jumping up and down to welcome you to the circus!

What You Can Add:
pom-poms

1. Cut a long strip of paper about 2 inches wide. Then pleat the strip. (To find out how to pleat, see page 3.)

2. Cut out a head for your clown, and glue it to one end of the pleated strip.

3. Add a funny face with cut-out shapes, and then add arms.

4. Give your clown a funny hat. Cut out a triangle. Then make pom-poms, using colorful paper circles. Or add real pom-poms.

Clown with real pom-poms

5. Make a colorful "box" for your clown to jump out of. Fold a sheet of colored paper in half the short way. Decorate it with cut-out shapes.

6. Use the school glue to glue one end of the pleated strip inside the box, as shown.

glue

7. Fold up your clown along the creases in the strip. Then fold down the clown's head inside the box.

8. Now open up the box, and let your clown jump out!

Here's More!

Turn your Jumping Clown into a card. Write a greeting inside, close it up, and give it to a friend!

Surprise!
Happy Birthday!

Friendly Lion

A circus lion should roar, but this big cat is as gentle as a little kitty!

To make your lion's face and mane

What You Need:
small paper cup   mug

1. Use the mug to trace a circle onto orange paper. Use the paper cup to trace a small circle onto yellow paper. Then cut out both circles. The yellow circle is your lion's face. The orange circle is its mane.

2. Cut out two small ears. Glue each ear to your lion's face. Then gently squeeze together the sides of each ear between your fingertips so they stand up.

3. Glue your lion's face to the mane.

4. Make your lion's mane shaggy. Cut fringes all around the orange circle. (To find out how, see page 3.) Then fluff the mane with your fingers.

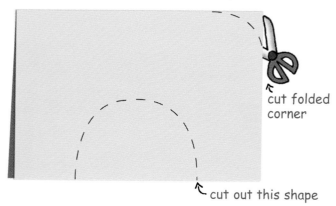

To make your lion's body

cut folded corner

cut out this shape

5. Cut out eyes, eyebrows, a nose, a mouth, and whiskers. Then glue them onto your lion's face.

6. Fold a piece of yellow paper in half the short way. Then cut out a shape like the one shown from the edges opposite the fold. Use your scissors to round off one end of the folded corners.

7. Glue your lion's head to the body. Add your lion's tail! Now fold out your lion's feet so your lion will stand up!

What else can you find at the circus? Turn the page to see!

High-wire Act

Look up—way, way up! The acrobat is balancing on the tightrope!

What You Can Add:
yarn tape markers

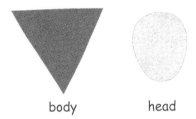

body   head

arms   legs   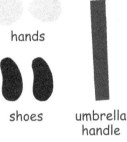 hands / shoes   umbrella handle

1. For your acrobat's body, cut out a paper triangle. Make an oval for her head.

2. Cut thin strips for arms and legs. Make small circles for hands and small ovals for shoes. Make a handle for the acrobat's umbrella, too.

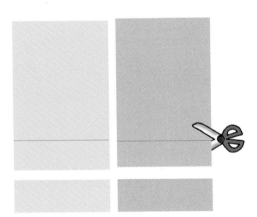

3. Make a pleated skirt for your acrobat and a pleated umbrella for her to hold. Cut two paper strips, each about 2 inches wide.

4. Pleat each strip of paper, making little folds. (To find out how to pleat, see page 3.)

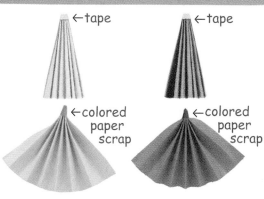

←tape ←tape

←colored paper scrap ←colored paper scrap

5. Close up each pleated strip. Tape one side of each strip, as shown. Fan out the other side. Cover the tape by gluing on a scrap of colored paper.

6. Put your acrobat together on a sheet of paper. Use your school glue to glue down her skirt and umbrella, and the glue stick for the other pieces.

7. Give your acrobat a face and some yarn hair. Glue a piece of yarn across the paper, beneath her feet.

Now your acrobat is balancing up on the high wire!

Up, Up, and Away!

Wouldn't you like to ride in a hot-air balloon?

What You Can Add:

yarn or string

dried pasta, beads, buttons, glitter, or other decorations

small paper cup

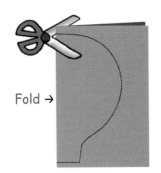

Fold →

1. To make your hot-air balloon, fold a sheet of paper in half the short way. Then cut out a shape like this, starting at the fold, and open it up.

2. Now make the bask for your balloon. Cu out a shape like thi

3. Decorate your basket and balloon. Cut out zigzags, stripes, and wavy shapes in different colors. You can make triangles, squares, and rectangles, too.

4. What else can you use to decorate your hot-air balloc How about some curly pasta colored beads, or buttons? Use school glue to add them to your balloon.

5. Cut two equal-sized pieces of yarn. Use school glue to stick them to the back of your balloon and basket.

6. Cut another piece of yarn. Glue it to the back of your balloon, near the top, as shown.

7. When the glue is dry, tape the string hanging from the balloon to a window, and let your hot-air balloon sway in the breeze!

Here's More!

Make a basket for your balloon that fits around a small paper cup, if you'd like. Try making some passengers to put inside. Then give them a ride!

FEATHERED FRIENDS
Wonderful Woven Egg

What kind of bird do you think will hatch out of this colorful egg?

What You Can Add:
Bits and scraps of yarn, ribbon, and paper

1. Cut an egg shape from a sheet of colored paper (you pick the color).

2. Fold your egg in half the short way. Starting at the fold, cut slits into the egg. Be careful not to cut all the way to the ends of the open sides. Reopen the egg.

3. Now cut thin strips of paper of different colors. Try making them different shapes—straight, wavy, or zigzag.

4. Weave each strip over and under each slit.

5. Glue down the ends each strip, using yo glue stick. Trim the ends of the strips i they hang off the e

6. Your egg needs a nest! Cut a sheet of paper into a nest shape.

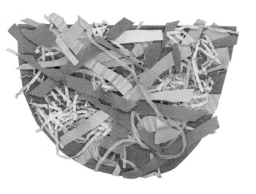

7. Cut lots of paper strips from scraps. Glue them to the nest. Add bits of yarn, ribbon, and other kinds of paper, too.

8. Place your egg behind your nest and glue it. Now your egg is snug and warm!

Peck, peck! Turn the page to see who will hatch out of this egg!

Whirly Birdies

These colorful birds love to swoop and soar in the breeze.

What You Can Add:
yarn

1. To make a whirly birdy, cut out different paper shapes: big and little triangles, half circles, ovals, and more!

2. Play with putting the shapes together in different ways to make a bird.

3. Give your whirly birdy fancy feathers by making curls, pleats, zigzags, fringes, or spirals. (See page 3 to find out how.)

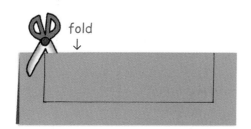

fold ↓

4. Make a frame for your whirly birdy to fly in. Fold a sheet of paper in half the long way. Starting on the fold, cut out a window.

5. Then unfold the paper and decorate your frame.

6. Glue a piece of yarn to the back of your bird. Glue the other end to your frame. Let the glue dry for a few minutes.

Now watch your whirly bird swoop and soar!

Purdy Bird Mask

Pretend you're a bird when you wear this fine-feathered mask!

Extras That You Need:

7- or 8-inch
  paper plate

unsharpened pencil

glitter (optional)

tape

1. Cut a wedge shape like this from the paper plate.

2. Fold the paper plate in half the long way. Cut out two eyeholes along the fold, and then reopen it. (Ask a grown-up for help, if you need it.)

3. Cut a beak shape and fold it up.

4. To make some feathers, fringe the rim of the plate on each side of the beak. (To find out how to fringe, see page 3.)

5. Give your bird more feathers! Cut out feather shapes from your paper.

6. Now fringe the sides of each feather. Be careful not to cut all the way to the middle.

dabs of glue

7. Dab some glue on the back of each feather, just along the middle. Then stick the feathers on your mask (away from the eyes and beak) and gently fluff the fringes.

8. Add glitter to make your Purdy Bird sparkle, if you like. For a handle, glue an unsharpened pencil to the back of your mask with school glue. Or tape it in place.

Happy Hats

When is your birthday? Here's a party hat that's perfect to top off your special day. Or you can use these hats for happy play any day.

Extras That You Need:

large paper plate

two paper clips

hole punch (optional)

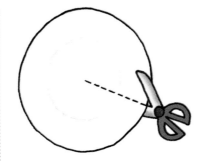

1. Cut a slit into the center of a paper plate like this.

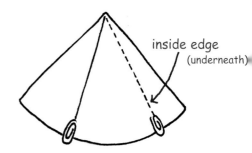

inside edge (underneath)

2. Hold the plate on your head, and overlap the cut parts until they fit like a hat. Use two paper clips to hold the shape together. Then take off your hat. (Ask someone to help, if you need it.)

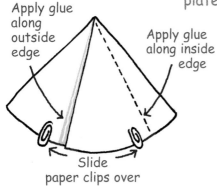

Apply glue along outside edge

Apply glue along inside edge

Slide paper clips over

3. Slide one paper clip over at a time and apply a thin line of school glue along each edge. Slide the paper clips back in place. Then let the glue dry.

4. Now it's time to decorate your hat! (Paint your hat first, if you like.) Here are some ideas to try:

▸ Add different-colored shapes to your hat. Cut out triangles, squiggles, spirals, and squares!

▸ Make some fancy flowers.

▸ Use a hole punch to make polka dots.

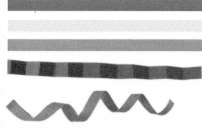

5. To add colorful streamers, cut lots of thin paper strips. Use different colors. Pleat or curl the streamers, if you like. (See page 3.)

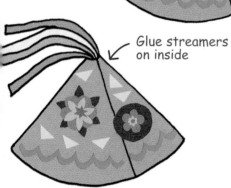

Glue streamers on inside

6. Carefully cut off the tip of your hat to make a small hole. Push the ends of the streamers through the hole, and glue them to the inside of your hat.

When does the party start?

Cozy Collage Quilt

Time for bed! This cozy quilt will keep you snug as a bug!

1. Cut your colored paper into shapes that are about the same size. Squares or triangles will work well.

2. Now decorate your shapes.

3. Pick a sheet of colored paper. On your paper, place the shapes in different ways to make a pattern.

4. When you like how the shapes look, glue them to your paper.

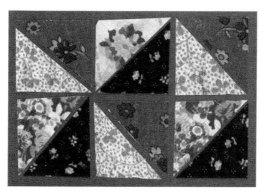

Here's More!
Try making a quilt using fabric scraps, instead of paper.

Doesn't your collage quilt look warm and cozy?

More Fun with Collage!

Try these ideas to create other great collage projects.

There are so many more collage pictures you can make! How about a penguin sliding on a shiny foil skating rink? Or a camel in a sandpaper desert stopping for a drink?

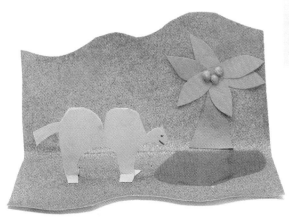

No part of this publication may be reproduced in whole or in part, or stored in a retrieval system, or transmitted in any form or by any means, electronic, mechanical, photocopying, recording, or otherwise, without written permission of the publisher. For information regarding permission, write to Scholastic Inc., Attention: Permissions Department, 555 Broadway, New York, NY 10012.

ISBN 0-439-33619-8

Designed by Julie Mullarkey   Art created by Julie Mullarkey and Deborah Schecter

Copyright © 2002 by Scholastic Inc.
All rights reserved. Published by Scholastic Inc.
SCHOLASTIC and associated logos are trademarks and/or registered trademarks of Scholastic Inc.

12 11 10 9 8 7 6 5 4 3 2 1   1 2 3 4 5 6/0
Printed in the U.S.A.
First Scholastic printing, January 2002